GODS AND GODDESSES OF ANCIENT GREECE

HADES
God of the Underworld

Written by Teri Temple
and Maria Koran
Illustrated by Robert Squier

MEDIA ENHANCED BOOKS
AV2 BY WEIGL
ADDED VALUE • AUDIO VISUAL

www.av2books.com

AV² provides enriched content that supplements and complements this book. Weigl's AV² books strive to create inspired learning and engage young minds in a total learning experience.

Your AV² Media Enhanced books come alive with...

Audio
Listen to sections of the book read aloud.

Key Words
Study vocabulary, and complete a matching word activity.

Video
Watch informative video clips.

Quizzes
Test your knowledge.

Embedded Weblinks
Gain additional information for research.

Slide Show
View images and captions, and prepare a presentation.

Try This!
Complete activities and hands-on experiments.

... and much, much more!

Go to **www.av2books.com**, and enter this book's unique code.

BOOK CODE

X428566

AV² by Weigl brings you media enhanced books that support active learning.

Published by AV² by Weigl
350 5th Avenue, 59th Floor
New York, NY 10118
Website: www.av2books.com

Library of Congress Cataloging-in-Publication Data

Names: Temple, Teri, author.
Title: Hades / Teri Temple.
Description: New York : AV² by Weigl, 2016. | Series: Gods and goddesses of ancient Greece | Includes index.
Identifiers: LCCN 2016002888 (print) | LCCN 2016004272 (ebook) | ISBN 9781489646439 (hard cover : alk. paper) | ISBN 9781489650429 (soft cover : alk. paper) | ISBN 9781489646446 (Multi-User eBook)
Subjects: LCSH: Hades (Greek deity)--Juvenile literature. | Mythology, Greek--Juvenile literature. | Gods, Greek--Juvenile literature.
Classification: LCC BL820.P58 T46 2016 (print) | LCC BL820.P58 (ebook) | DDC 292.2/113--dc23
LC record available at http://lccn.loc.gov/2016002888

Printed in Brainerd, Minnesota, United States
1 2 3 4 5 6 7 8 9 0 20 19 18 17 16

072016
070416

Project Coordinator: Warren Rylands
Art Director: Terry Paulhus

Every reasonable effort has been made to trace ownership and to obtain permission to reprint copyright material. The publishers would be pleased to have any errors or omissions brought to their attention so that they may be corrected in subsequent printings.

Weigl acknowledges Getty Images and iStock as its primary image suppliers for this title.

CONTENTS

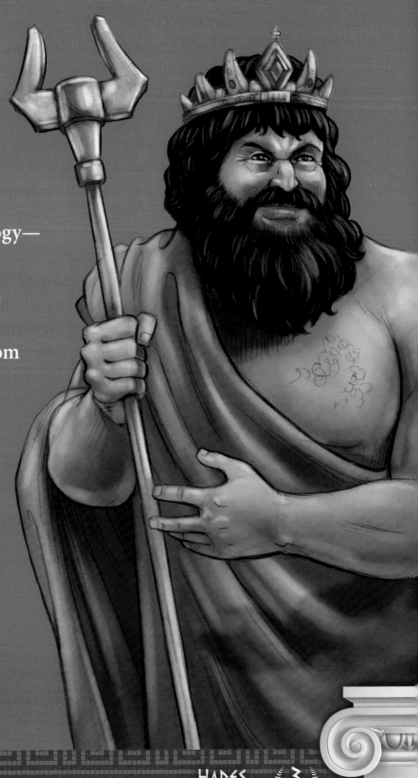

HADES 3

INTRODUCTION

Long ago in **ancient Greece** and Rome, most people believed that gods and goddesses ruled their world. Storytellers shared the adventures of these gods to help explain all the mysteries in life. The gods were immortal, meaning they lived forever. Their stories were full of love and tragedy, fearsome monsters, brave heroes, and struggles for power. The storytellers wove aspects of Greek customs and beliefs into the tales. Some stories told of the creation of the world and the origins of the gods. Others helped explain natural events such as earthquakes and storms. People believed the tales, which over time became myths.

The ancient Greeks and Romans **worshiped** the gods by building temples and statues in their honor. They felt the gods would protect and guide them. People passed down the myths through the generations by word of mouth. Later, famous poets such as Homer and Hesiod wrote them down. Today, these myths give us a unique look at what life was like in ancient Greece more than 2,000 years ago.

ANCIENT GREEK SOCIETIES

In ancient Greece, cities, towns, and their surrounding farmlands were called city-states. These city-states each had their own governments. They made their own laws. The individual city-states were very independent. They never joined to become one whole nation. They did, however, share a common language, religion, and culture.

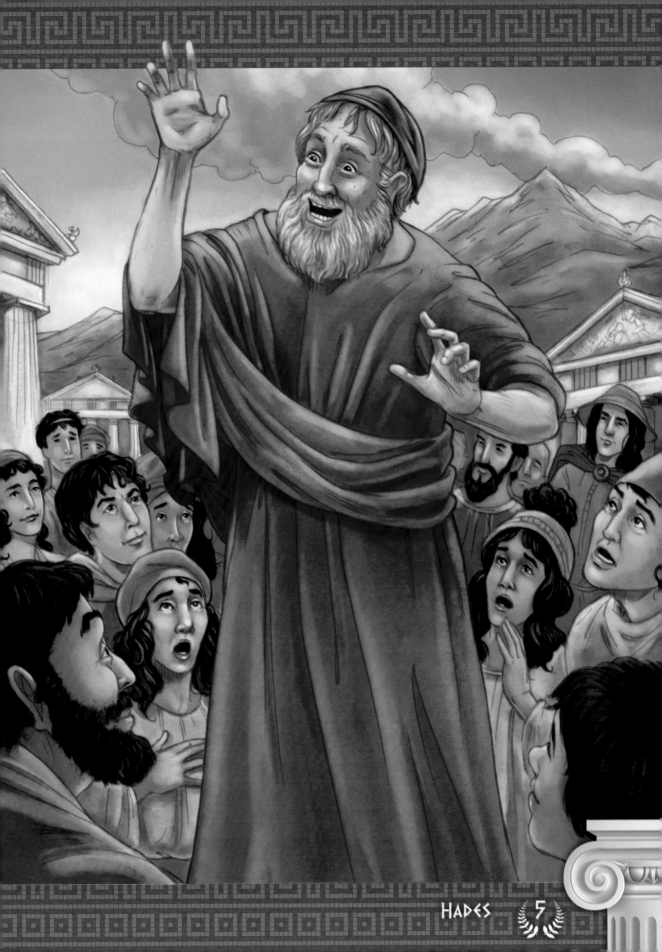

CHARACTERS AND PLACES

Mount Olympus
The mountaintop home of the 12 Olympic gods

Aegean Sea

ANCIENT
GREECE

CRETE

Olympian Gods
Demeter, Hermes, Hephaestus, Aphrodite, Ares, Hera, Zeus, Poseidon, Athena, Apollo, Artemis, and Dionysus

Titans
The 12 children of Gaea and Cronus; godlike giants that are said to represent the forces of nature

Underworld
The land of the dead; ruled over by Hades; must cross the river Styx to gain entrance

Cerberus (SUR-bur-uhs)
Giant three-headed dog that guards
the entrance to the underworld

Cronus (CROW-nus)
A Titan who ruled the world;
married to Rhea and their children
became the first six Olympic gods

Cyclopes (SIGH-clopes)
One-eyed giants; children
of Gaea and Uranus

Demeter (di-MEE-tur)
Goddess of the harvest;
mother of Persephone

Erinyes (ih-RIN-ee-eez)
The three serpent-haired
goddesses of vengeance; punished
the wicked in the underworld

Fates (FEYTS)
The three goddesses of fate; they
determine when life begins and
ends; daughters of Zeus

Sisyphus (SIS-i-fuhs)
Human whose punishment in the
underworld was to forever push a
boulder up a hill

Heracles (HER-uh-kleez)
Son of Zeus; hero of Greek myths

Hestia (HES-tee-uh)
Goddess of the hearth; daughter
of Cronus and Rhea

Orpheus (OHR-fee-uhs)
Human who traveled to
the underworld to rescue
his wife Eurydice

**Persephone
(per-SEF-uh-nee)**
Daughter of the goddess Demeter;
married to Hades

Poseidon (puh-SY-duhn)
God of the sea and earthquakes;
brother to Zeus

**Pirithous
(py-RITH-oh-uhs)**
Tried to kidnap Persephone and
ended up trapped in the
underworld by Hades

Gaea (JEE-uh)
Mother Earth and one of the first
elements born to Chaos; mother of
the Titans, Cyclopes,
and Hecatoncheires

Zeus (ZOOS)
Supreme ruler of the heavens and
weather and of the gods who lived
on Mount Olympus; youngest son of
Cronus and Rhea; married to Hera;
father of many gods and heroes

THE GOD OF THE UNDERWORLD

At the beginning of time there was only darkness. Out of the darkness came Gaea, or Mother Earth. The heavens and the sky followed. Together they would become the parents of a race of giants known as the Titans. The Titans represented the different forces of nature. It was from these giants that the story of the Olympic gods began.

The youngest Titan was Cronus. He challenged his father to become the supreme ruler of the universe. With the help of his brothers and sisters, Cronus defeated his father and banned him from the earth. Cronus and his wife Rhea gave birth to the first gods. Cronus was worried that his children would try to overthrow him, just as he had done to his father. So after each child was born, he swallowed the child up. But Rhea figured out a way to trick Cronus. She hid the sixth child on an island after he was born. Instead of a child, Cronus swallowed a stone wrapped in a blanket.

On the island, the baby grew up to be Zeus. He wanted to rescue his brothers and sisters. Zeus's wife Metis helped him figure out a plan. Metis gave Cronus a drink. He thought it would make him incredibly strong. Instead, it made him throw up. First he threw up the stone and then his children—all in one piece! The three sisters were Hestia, Demeter, and Hera. The two brothers were Poseidon and Hades. They were all thrilled to be free.

The six brothers and sisters now had a battle on their hands. If they wanted to defeat their father, they needed some help. Mother Earth convinced Zeus to release her other children, the Cyclopes and the Hecatoncheires, from an underworld prison. The Cyclopes were mighty, one-eyed giants. The Hecatoncheires were monsters. Each had 100 arms and 50 heads. They would be wonderful partners to the gods.

The Cyclopes were great **blacksmiths**. They created weapons for the battle. For Zeus they made a mighty thunderbolt. With it he could shake the universe. For Poseidon they formed a trident. This was a three-pronged spear that could divide the seas. For Hades they created a helmet of darkness. It allowed him to move invisibly among his enemies.

The battle would last ten long years. Defeat finally came when Hades used his helmet to sneak into the Titans' camp. Poseidon distracted the Titans with the power of his trident. Hades stole all of their weapons. Zeus then blasted the Titans with his thunderbolt. The crushing blow came as the Cyclopes and Hecatoncheires battered the Titans with boulders. With the universe nearly destroyed, the Titans gave up the fight.

Peace fell upon Earth. The universe was divided among the three brothers. Zeus became the king of all gods and ruler of the heavens. Poseidon was made god of the seas. Hades was made god of the underworld.

Even though he was ruler of the seas, Poseidon lived on Mount Olympus. Hades was the only brother who was not one of the 12 Olympians.

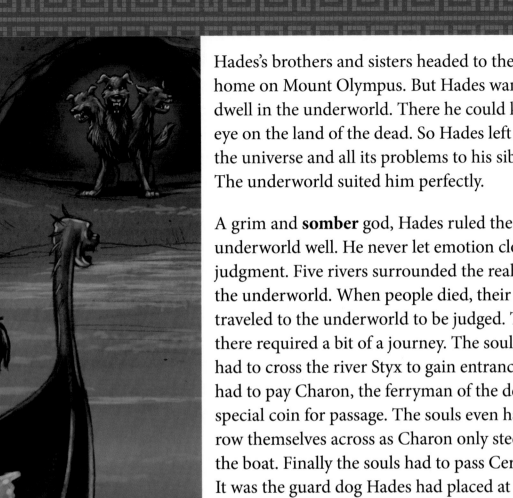

Hades's brothers and sisters headed to their new home on Mount Olympus. But Hades wanted to dwell in the underworld. There he could keep an eye on the land of the dead. So Hades left ruling the universe and all its problems to his siblings. The underworld suited him perfectly.

A grim and **somber** god, Hades ruled the underworld well. He never let emotion cloud his judgment. Five rivers surrounded the realm of the underworld. When people died, their **souls** traveled to the underworld to be judged. To get there required a bit of a journey. The souls first had to cross the river Styx to gain entrance. They had to pay Charon, the ferryman of the dead, a special coin for passage. The souls even had to row themselves across as Charon only steered the boat. Finally the souls had to pass Cerberus. It was the guard dog Hades had placed at the entrance. Cerberus was a huge three-headed beast that never slept. It made sure the souls of the dead never escaped. It also did not let the living enter.

HESTIA

Hestia was like her brother Hades. She did not want the attention most gods received on Mount Olympus. She was the gentle goddess of the hearth. A hearth is the area before a fireplace. Hestia chose to spend her days sitting beside the palace fireplace. Her job was to make sure the Olympus fire never went out. Hestia protected all of the homes on Earth. Humans and gods alike honored her.

Once the souls passed Cerberus they reached a fork in the road. It was here they would learn their fate. Each soul had to face the three judges of the dead. They would decide in which level of the underworld the soul would reside for all of time. Sometimes other gods would step in and help decide where a soul should go. But Hades never did.

The ancient Greeks believed that the underworld was beneath the earth. It was made up of three levels. One was only for the souls of outstanding people, like those of the heroes. It was known as Elysium Fields. Here souls lived forever in paradise. Another level was Tartarus. It was home to those who had been evil. It was located far beneath the underworld. Only the very wicked were sent there. Hades had the Erinyes give out punishment to these souls. Most souls, however, went to a dull and dreary place called Asphodel Fields. It was a middle ground for the most common souls. It was neither good nor bad. Hades ruled over a busy kingdom.

THE ERINYES

The Erinyes were the three daughters of Mother Earth with serpents on their heads. They were powerful goddesses of revenge who lived in the underworld. But they traveled to Earth to seek out humans who committed terrible crimes. The Erinyes carried whips to punish the wicked and drive them to madness. They especially hated murderers.

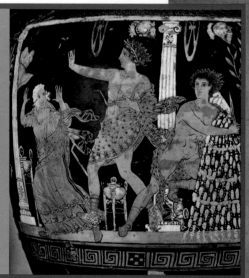

The underworld was full of souls and the attendants of Hades. Still Hades was lonely. He wanted a bride to help rule over his kingdom. The tale of how Hades found his queen was a sad one indeed.

Demeter was Hades's sister and goddess of the harvest. She had a beautiful daughter named Persephone who had grown up on Mount Olympus. Several of the gods wanted to marry Persephone. She was so lovely and graceful that even Hades took notice of her. He immediately fell in love and wanted her as his bride. But Demeter was not ready to give her up. Hades knew Demeter would never let him have Persephone. So he hatched a plan to carry her off.

One day as Persephone gathered flowers in the meadow, a huge crack opened up in the ground. Out came a dark chariot pulled by fierce black stallions. Holding the reins was Hades. He kidnapped Persephone and dragged her screaming down into the underworld.

VIRGO CONSTELLATION

Virgo is the sixth **constellation** in the **zodiac**. You can find it in the southern sky between Leo, the lion, and Libra, the scales. It was identified as a young maiden carrying a sheaf of wheat. The ancient Greeks believed that it was Persephone, the harvest maiden. One of the brightest stars in the sky is Spica. It is part of the Virgo constellation.

Demeter was terribly upset when she discovered that Persephone was gone. She wandered Earth in search of her. Demeter refused to let anything grow until she found her daughter. She even asked Zeus for help. In order to return **fertility** to Earth, Zeus knew he needed to get involved. He sent Hermes down to the underworld to fetch Persephone. Hermes found Persephone in the gloomy palace of the dead. She was as silent and somber as her husband Hades. Persephone leapt to her feet when she spied Hermes. Hope filled her heart that she might be returned to her mother.

Hades had hoped to lure Persephone into staying. But he knew he could not refuse Zeus's command. Instead, he tricked her into eating a single pomegranate seed. According to the laws of the Fates, anyone who ate food in the underworld could never return to the land of the living.

Hades was often shown holding a key, representing that he was the jailer of the dead.

Zeus had to follow the rules of the Fates. The Fates were three of his daughters. As goddesses, their role was to spin and cut the thread of life. With it they determined the paths of people's lives. However, Zeus managed to work out a deal. Persephone would be allowed to return to Earth to live with her mother for eight months of the year. During that time, Demeter would allow the world to flourish. This would provide the **crops** for the humans on Earth.

The final four months Persephone would return to the land of the dead. There she would rule with Hades as queen of the underworld. Persephone was not happy about the deal. Demeter's grief brought winter during the four months Persephone was gone. The rules of the Fates were final, though. So the mother and daughter patiently awaited the return of spring each year. Hades even became known as the god of Earth's fertility. By allowing Persephone to spend part of the year with her mother, he made sure there would be a good harvest.

THE FOUR SEASONS

Demeter was the goddess of crops and harvest. The ancient Greeks believed she controlled the growing seasons. After her daughter Persephone married Hades, Persephone went to live in the underworld for the winter. The Greeks thought Demeter's grief caused the weather to get bad. Winter was when all of the crops died. Demeter's happiness when her daughter returned brought spring back. The myth of Persephone explained the cycle of the four seasons.

Hades was kept busy dealing with all the problems death created. Theseus and his friend Pirithous were two of the troublemakers Hades dealt with. Hades met them when they traveled to the underworld to kidnap his bride Persephone. Theseus was just along to return a favor. It was Pirithous who wanted to marry the queen of the underworld.

Theseus and Pirithous fought their way through all of the challenges in Hades's realm. Once they found themselves in Hades's palace they told him they had come for Persephone. Hades found this all very amusing. But he did not intend to let them succeed with their plan. Hades invited the men to take a seat and discuss it. Theseus and Pirithous sat down and snakes appeared. They held the two men tightly to the chair. Hades had tricked them into sitting on the Chair of Forgetfulness. They remained stuck there for years.

SISYPHUS

Sisyphus was also a clever human who tried to cheat death. When Zeus found out, he sent him to Hades for punishment. Sisyphus would spend every day trying to roll an enormous boulder up a hill. He never reached the top, though. The boulder would always roll back to the bottom.

The hero Heracles discovered Theseus and Pirithous while trying to complete one of his 12 labors. These were tasks he had been ordered to complete. He had traveled to the underworld to convince Hades to let him borrow Cerberus. Heracles was able to free Theseus. But Hades refused to let the man who tried to kidnap his wife go. Pirithous was destined to spend all of time there.

Two other humans shared a similar fate. Orpheus loved his wife Eurydice. He was very sad when she died from a snakebite. He could not live without her. So he too traveled to the underworld to try and win her back. As a gifted musician, Orpheus was able to charm his way into the realm with his music.

Persephone showed favor to the young lovers and agreed to let them leave. There was just one condition. Orpheus could not look back on Eurydice until they were safely past the borders of the underworld. Orpheus agreed. But as they neared the end of their journey, he could not resist checking on his wife. As soon as he turned, Eurydice was whisked back below. Orpheus had to spend the rest of his life alone.

Because of his association with it, the underworld itself is sometimes called Hades.

There were many steps to getting into the underworld. But the most important involved burying the dead. Hades only allowed those souls who had received a proper burial into the underworld. That is why the ancient Greeks made sure to bury people in a certain way. There were three important steps involved.

First the relatives, mainly women, washed the body. Next the body was rubbed with oils and placed on a high bed in the house. Friends and relatives would come to **mourn** the dead and pay their respects. Mourning the dead was a common theme in ancient Greek art.

The rituals continued with a funeral procession. This is when the body is taken on a path to the burial site. Just before dawn, the body was either buried in the ground or burned into ash. The relatives had to remember to place a coin in the mouth of the dead. The soul would need this coin to give to Charon. It would buy the soul passage across the river Styx.

ANCIENT GREEK ART

In 323 BC, Alexander the Great died. He was an important king of the ancient world. For the next 200 years, ancient Greek culture ruled much of the civilized world. The arts flourished. Greek sculptors and painters became skilled in making realistic art. Much of what we know about that time comes from the scenes painted on pottery. Artists portrayed images of mythology and daily life.

The ancient Greeks placed statues near the burial mounds to mark their graves. This made sure that those who died were not forgotten. The dead would always be alive in others' memories.

Hades was honored in the ancient Greeks' funeral ceremonies. A few temples or shrines were dedicated in his name. And every 100 years, Hades was honored at festivals called the Secular Games.

Hades would continue even after Rome conquered Greece. During the sixth and seventh centuries the Romans adopted much of the Greeks' culture. The Roman god of the dead became known as Pluto.

Unfortunately for Hades, the afterlife was not something humans wanted to think about. The common folk did not have much to look forward to and the wicked had much to fear! The stories of the other Olympic gods were full of excitement and adventure. But Hades and his awesome strength in the underworld will always be important in Greek mythology.

It was considered unlucky to say Hades's name out loud, so the Greeks sometimes called him by other names, such as Pluto, as well.

HADES 29

PRINCIPAL GODS OF GREEK MYTHOLOGY— A FAMILY TREE

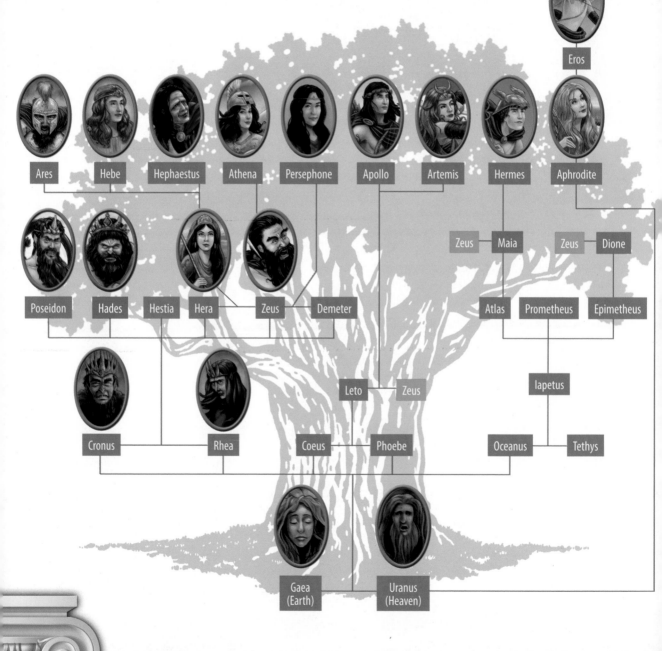

Eros

Ares | Hebe | Hephaestus | Athena | Persephone | Apollo | Artemis | Hermes | Aphrodite

Zeus | Maia | Zeus | Dione

Poseidon | Hades | Hestia | Hera | Zeus | Demeter

Atlas | Prometheus | Epimetheus

Iapetus

Cronus | Rhea | Leto | Zeus | Coeus | Phoebe | Oceanus | Tethys

Gaea (Earth) | Uranus (Heaven)

KEY WORDS

ancient Greece: historical period that lasted from about 800 to 323 BC, during which many advancements were made in politics, art, philosophy, and science

blacksmiths: people who make or repair items made of iron

constellation: a group of stars that creates a shape in the sky and has been given a name

crops: plants grown by farmers

fertility: being able to support the growth of many plants

mourn: feeling or showing great sadness when someone has died

somber: gloomy, sad, and very serious

souls: the spiritual part of people, in many religions the soul is believed to live forever

worshiped: showed respect and honor, often through prayer or other religious acts

zodiac: imaginary area in the sky that the planets, Sun, and Moon appear to travel through. The zodiac is divided into 12 parts that each have a special name and symbol, believed by some people to influence events

INDEX

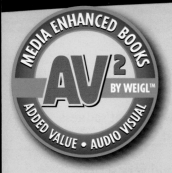

Log on to www.av2books.com

AV² by Weigl brings you media enhanced books that support active learning. Go to www.av2books.com, and enter the special code found on page 2 of this book. You will gain access to enriched and enhanced content that supplements and complements this book. Content includes video, audio, weblinks, quizzes, a slide show, and activities.

AV² Online Navigation

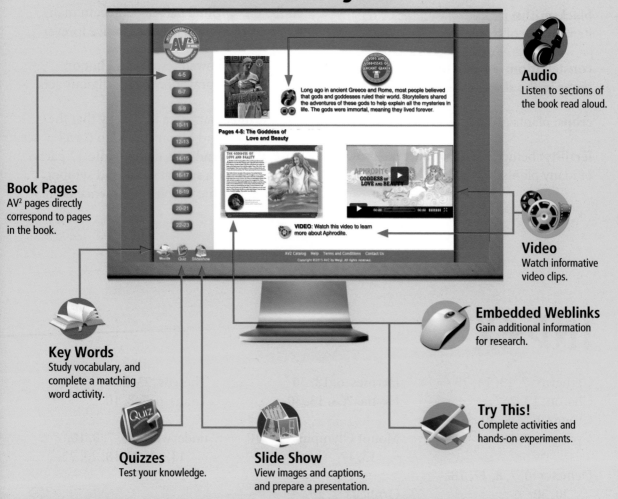

Audio
Listen to sections of the book read aloud.

Book Pages
AV² pages directly correspond to pages in the book.

Video
Watch informative video clips.

Embedded Weblinks
Gain additional information for research.

Key Words
Study vocabulary, and complete a matching word activity.

Try This!
Complete activities and hands-on experiments.

Quizzes
Test your knowledge.

Slide Show
View images and captions, and prepare a presentation.

AV² was built to bridge the gap between print and digital. We encourage you to tell us what you like and what you want to see in the future.

Sign up to be an AV² Ambassador at www.av2books.com/ambassador.

Due to the dynamic nature of the Internet, some of the URLs and activities provided as part of AV² by Weigl may have changed or ceased to exist. AV² by Weigl accepts no responsibility for any such changes. All media enhanced books are regularly monitored to update addresses and sites in a timely manner. Contact AV² by Weigl at 1-866-649-3445 or av2books@weigl.com with any questions, comments, or feedback.